T0209491

A CATHOLIC GUIDE to PERSONAL INVESTING

Peace
Through Stewardship

Seth C. Anderson, PhD

WESTBOW
PRESS®
A DIVISION OF THOMAS NELSON
& ZONDERVAN

WestBow Press books may be ordered through booksellers or by contacting:

WestBow Press
A Division of Thomas Nelson & Zondervan
1663 Liberty Drive
Bloomington, IN 47403
www.westbowpress.com
1 (866) 928-1240

ISBN: 978-1-9736-5248-9 (sc)
ISBN: 978-1-9736-5249-6 (e)

Library of Congress Control Number: 2019901093

Print information available on the last page.

WestBow Press rev. date: 2/15/2019

It is written:
"One does not live by bread alone,
but by every word that comes forth
from the mouth of God."
—Matthew 4:4

Contents

PART III
Morally Responsible Investing

PART IV
Addressing Our Catholic Investment Responsibilities

Preface

As is seen in the Catechism of the Catholic Church, "it belongs to the laity to seek the kingdom of God by engaging in temporal affairs and directing them according to God's will."[1] Investing is one such affair that can affect our ability to serve our Lord as it influences how we touch human life, both now and in the future.

We Catholics are blessed to have many Church-related sources that give us both practical and moral guidance for our investing. This book draws from a variety of these offerings to help deal with the numerous issues confronting us in this endeavor. The work is divided into four parts:

Part I focuses on several faith-related matters relevant to investing as they appear in Scripture, the Catechism, and the writings of various saints and others. The topics include thanksgiving, stewardship, prudence, anxiety, greed, temperance, and prayer, all of which can impact our investing efforts.

Part II presents an overview of investing principles and facts to be considered when managing a portfolio. Herein, the four primary purposes are as follows: (a) to explain basic investing, (b) to familiarize readers with the return characteristics of different types of investments, (c) to show how various expenses impact investment returns, and (d) to address the issue of whether you should rely primarily on professional help or on your own efforts for making investment decisions.

Part III addresses morally responsible investing. This section draws from the pastoral letter *Economic Justice for All* and summarizes the United States Conference of Catholic Bishops'

---

[1] *Catechism of the Catholic Church* (Washington, DC: USCCB Publishing, 1997), 898.

(USCCB) Socially Responsible Investment Guidelines.[2] It also presents Professor Germain Grisez's position on investing in companies involved in questionable activities, as presented in his book Difficult Moral Questions.[3] The section concludes with a brief analysis of how investing in a business affects that firm.

The final part offers suggestions to help with both secular and faith-related challenges confronting us in our investment ventures. For example, we address how to temper investing with essentials such as stewardship and prudence as opposed to blindly following the investment practices often promoted by the investments industry. In another vein, this section addresses selecting investments that are harmonious with Church teachings. The four largest groups of Catholic-oriented mutual funds are then introduced. Next, several questions are addressed, including those about what will happen with your investments if you become incapacitated and what will happen with them when you die. The book concludes by revisiting Saint Padre Pio's prescription for eternal health, "Pray, Hope, and Don't Worry," as it pertains to investing.

In closing this introduction, I borrow a quote from Saint Francis de Sales: "As one great man of letters used to say: 'a good way to learn is to study, and a better way is to listen; but the best way of all is to teach.'"[4] Thus, in this attempt to provide you with useful investing perspectives and guidelines, I also seek to gain insights for my own investing in order to better serve our Lord.

---

[2] "Socially Responsible Investment Guidelines," United States Conference of Catholic Bishops, accessed August 15, 2017, http://www.usccb.org/about/financial-reporting/socially-responsible-investment-guidelines.cfm.
[3] Germain Grisez, *The Way of the Lord: Difficult Moral Questions*. Vol. 3 (New York: St. Paul's/Alba House, 1997).
[4] St. Francis de Sales, abridged by Madame Yvonne Stephan, *Introduction to the Devout Life* (Charlotte, NC: Tan Books and Publishers, 1990), xxiv.

PART I

Faith-Related Matters in Investing

Giving Thanks to God

Watch carefully then how you live ... giving thanks always and for
everything in the name of our Lord Jesus Christ to God the Father.
—Ephesians 5:15, 20

All that we have—our souls, lives, faith, families, vocations, and worldly wealth—are God's gifts to us, and we are to be thankful to Him for these blessings. Throughout the Scriptures, we see numerous examples of how we are to give *thanks* to God. As seen in Colossians 3:15–17, Paul states:

> 15 And let the peace of Christ control your hearts, the peace into which you were also called in one body. And be thankful.
>
> 16 Let the word of Christ dwell in you richly, as in all wisdom you teach and admonish one another, singing psalms, hymns, and spiritual songs with gratitude in your hearts to God.
>
> 17 And whatever you do, in word or in deed, do everything in the name of the Lord Jesus, giving thanks to God the Father through him.

When we attribute our blessings to ourselves rather than to God's generosity, we become self-centered, creating a myriad of problems for ourselves and for those around us. We are told about this in 2 Timothy 3:1–4:

> 1 But understand this: there will be terrifying times in the last days.
>
> 2 People will be self-centered and lovers of money, proud, haughty, abusive, disobedient to their parents, ungrateful, irreligious,
>
> 3 callous, implacable, slanderous, licentious, brutal, hating what is good,
>
> 4 traitors, reckless, conceited, lovers of pleasure rather than lovers of God …

Instead, as Paul writes in Ephesians 5:18-20, we are to give joyful thanks to the Lord for all of our blessings by being:

> 18 … filled with the Spirit,
>
> 19 addressing one another (in) psalms and hymns and spiritual songs, singing and playing to the Lord in your hearts,
>
> 20 giving thanks always and for everything in the name of our Lord Jesus Christ to God the Father.

Stewardship

Much will be required of the person entrusted with much,
and still more will be demanded of the person entrusted with more.
—Luke 12:48

God calls us to be good *stewards* of the blessings entrusted to us,
which include our time, talents, and material possessions. Yet we
often envision our time to be our own, and frequently we think of
our talents as ours since we strive to develop them. As well, we tend
to believe that we may do as we wish with our material possessions
because of legal title to them. However, they are only lent to us, as
we take nothing with us when we depart this world. At that time
we are called to account for how we have served God in managing
the blessings entrusted to us.[1]

Stewardship recognizes this and is our faith-based response in
answering the Lord's call to be worthy servants. In Genesis 43:16–
17 we are given an example of a good steward's doing as instructed:

> 16 When Joseph saw Benjamin with them, he told
> his head steward, "Take these men into the
> house, and have an animal slaughtered and
> prepared, for they are to dine with me at
> noon."

---

[1] Adapted from "Stewardship of Time and Talents" by the Most Reverend
Thomas J. Rodi. The original appeared on page 3 of *The Catholic Week*,
September 25, 2009.

17 Doing as Joseph had ordered, the steward
   conducted the men to Joseph's house.

Again, in Luke 12:40–43 we find one of the well-known references to stewardship:

40 You also must be prepared, for at an hour you do
   not expect, the Son of Man will come.

41 Then Peter said, "Lord, is this parable meant for
   us or for everyone?"

42 And the Lord replied, "Who, then, is the faithful
   and prudent steward whom the master will
   put in charge of his servants to distribute
   (the) food allowance at the proper time?

43 Blessed is that servant whom his master on
   arrival finds doing so."

In both instances, the stewards do what is required of them. Similarly, we must answer our Lord's call to be good stewards of our gifts. Doing so facilitates our ability to provide for ourselves and for those we are to serve. We are instructed to do this, as seen in 1 Peter 4:10: "As each one has received a gift, use it to serve one another as good stewards of God's varied grace."

Prudence

Good sense brings favor,
but the way of the faithless is their ruin.
The shrewd man does everything with prudence,
but the fool peddles folly.
—Proverbs 13:15–16

In the Catholic Encyclopedia, prudence is defined by Father Rickaby as "right reason applied to practice."[1] Being one of the four cardinal virtues, it can enable a person to effect suitable means for attaining a good purpose or avoiding an evil one.

Although prudence is a term that is not often heard in today's secular world, it is an important virtue. Its value is revealed throughout Scripture, as is seen in the book of Wisdom 8:5–7:

> 5 And if riches be a desirable possession in life, what is more rich than Wisdom, who produces all things?
>
> 6 And if prudence renders service, who in the world is a better craftsman than she?
>
> 7 Or if one loves justice, the fruits of her works are virtues;

---

[1] "Prudence," New Advent, accessed June 14, 2017. http://www.newadvent.org/cathen/12517b.htm. Father Rickaby was a British Jesuit of the pre–World War I era. This site contains the *Catholic Encyclopedia*.

For she teaches moderation and prudence, justice
and fortitude, and nothing in life is more
useful for men than these.

Prudence is essential for being a good steward in crafting life's many undertakings, including investing. The well-known parable of the talents in Matthew 25:15–18 speaks clearly to this issue. Herein, a man leaves on a journey, entrusting his possessions to his servants:

15 To one he gave five talents; to another, two; to a
third, one—to each according to his ability.
Then he went away. Immediately

16 the one who received five talents went and traded
with them, and made another five.

17 Likewise, the one who received two made
another two.

18 But the man who received one went off and dug
a hole in the ground and buried his master's
money.

Upon returning and seeing what the servants had done, the master was pleased with the first two and asked them to share in his joy. As for the third one, who had acted imprudently, the master said to him in Matthew 25:26: "You wicked, lazy servant!"

As seen in this parable, we are to be good stewards of the gifts God entrusts to us. Each of us is given time, talent, and material wealth, all of which we are to manage according to our abilities. We should do so in a prudent manner pleasing to our Lord.

4 Anxiety

Have no anxiety at all, but in everything,
by prayer and petition, with thanksgiving,
make your requests known to God.
—Philippians 4:6

According to *The American Heritage Dictionary of the English Language* anxious is being "worried and strained about some unexpected event or matter." We are told throughout Scripture to avoid anxiety. In Matthew 6:28–33 Jesus says:

28 Why are you anxious about clothes? Learn from the way the wild flowers grow. They do not work or spin.

29 But I tell you that not even Solomon in all his splendor was clothed like one of them.

30 If God so clothes the grass of the field, which grows today and is thrown into the oven tomorrow, will he not much more provide for you, O you of little faith?

31 So do not worry and say, "What are we to eat?" or "What are we to drink?" or "What are we to wear?"

32 All these things the pagans seek. Your heavenly Father knows that you need them all.

33 But seek first the kingdom (of God) and his righteousness, and all these things will be given you besides.

Yet, we often worry about our jobs, families, and health, among other things. Yes, our lives are full of uncertainties regardless of who we are or what we do. Nonetheless, our Lord tells us not to be anxious, but to choose faith in Him, as is seen in Luke 10:41–42:

41 The Lord said to her in reply, "Martha, Martha, you are anxious and worried about many things.

42 There is need of only one thing. Mary has chosen the better part and it will not be taken from her."

Even so, for many of us in today's world, our financial circumstances often generate varying degrees of anxiety. Perhaps this is because we place too much emphasis on financial matters. We must keep our material wealth in perspective, as is evidenced in Baruch 3:15–19:

15 Who has found the place of wisdom, who has entered into her treasuries?

16 Where are the rulers of the nations, they who lorded it over the wild beasts of the earth,

17 and made sport of the birds of the heavens: They who heaped up the silver and the gold in which men trust; of whose possessions there was no end?

18 They schemed anxiously for money, but there is no trace of their work:

19 They have vanished down into the nether world, and others have risen up in their stead.

Truly, our material wealth is only temporal and is not of the utmost importance. This being said, we are not relieved of our responsibilities to manage our gifts to the best of our abilities. The following quote from Saint Francis de Sales may be a good prescription for avoiding anxiety when managing our affairs in God's service:

> The solicitous care which ought to characterize our affairs is altogether different from a bothersome worry and anxiety over them. ... Therefore, be careful and diligent ... about all your affairs. Having confided them to you, God wishes you to have a great concern for them. But, if possible, do not be obsessed with them. Do not undertake them with distress, anxiety or frenzy. And, never rush into them, because too much eagerness disturbs reason and judgment, and even prevents our doing well what we are hurrying to do.[1]

---

[1] St. Francis de Sales, *Introduction to the Devout Life* (Charlotte, NC: Tan Books and Publishers, Inc., 1990), 155.

5

Greed

For gold has dazzled many,
and perverts the character of princes.
—Sirach 8:2

The above words hold true today as they did in antiquity. Such is seen in a past editorial letter by Professor Kuebler, who delineates how unbridled greed for profits and goods lies at the root of many of our problems. He posits that many of our economic and social problems are the result of a moral crisis caused by our worldliness. Although many blame Wall Street for its greed, Dr. Kuebler points out that Main Street itself is also largely at fault, as many people worship the idol of excessive consumption. Thus, our incessant desire for creature comforts and grand profits has largely contributed to our plight. He quotes Pope John Paul II, who says that we must look beyond ourselves:

> Christ alone can free man from what enslaves him
> to evil and selfishness: from the frantic search for
> material possessions, from the thirst for power and
> control over others and over things, from the illusion
> of easy success, from the frenzy of consumerism
> and hedonism, which ultimately destroy the human
> being.[1]

---

[1] Daniel Kuebler, "The Mess Money Made," *The National Catholic Register,* May 10-16, 2009, 7.

Jesus addresses the issue of greed in the parable of the rich man in Luke 12:15–21:

> 15 Then he said to the crowd, "Take care to guard against all greed, for though one may be rich, one's life does not consist of possessions."
>
> 16 Then he told them a parable. "There was a rich man whose land produced a bountiful harvest.
>
> 17 He asked himself, 'What shall I do, for I do not have space to store my harvest?'
>
> 18 And he said, 'This is what I shall do: I shall tear down my barns and build larger ones. There I shall store all my grain and other goods
>
> 19 and I shall say to myself, "Now as for you, you have so many good things stored up for many years, rest, eat, drink, be merry!"'
>
> 20 But God said to him, 'You fool, this night your life will be demanded of you; and the things you have prepared, to whom will they belong?'
>
> 21 Thus will it be for the one who stores up treasure for himself but is not rich in what matters to God."

God gives each of us gifts to manage, as is seen in the Parable of the Talents, and He expects us to do so wisely. Using our God-given talents to augment our investment assets is not being greedy as long as we seek to manage them, not for ourselves, but for the purpose of serving God.

Temperance

For the love of money is the root of all evils,
and some people in their desire for it
have strayed from the faith
and have pierced themselves with many pains.
—I Timothy 6:10

In contrast to greed, the moral virtue of *temperance* as seen in the *Catholic Catechism*:

> … moderates the attraction of pleasures and provides balance in the use of created goods. It ensures the will's mastery over instincts and keeps desires within the limits of what is honorable.[1]

Similarly, Monsignor Charles Murphy states that:

> According to Saint Thomas Aquinas, temperance gives order and balance to our life. It arises from a serenity of spirit within oneself. This reasonable norm allows us to walk gently upon the earth. Temperance teaches us to cherish and enjoy the good things of life while respecting natural limits.[2]

---

[1] Catholic Church, *Catechism of the Catholic Church*, 2nd ed. (Washington, DC: Libreria Editrice Vaticana, 2012), para. 1809.

[2] Monsignor Charles Murphy, "The Good Life from a Catholic Perspective: The Problem of Consumption," accessed October 24, 2018, http://www.squidinkbooks.com/omosclc/ppt/Creation/Good.Life.pdf.

Thus, when we approach investing, we must temper our desire for material possessions and worldly recognition. Rather, as the Catechism reveals:

> The temperate person directs the sensitive appetites toward what is good and maintains a healthy discretion: "Do not follow your inclination and strength, walking according to the desires of your heart."[3] Temperance is often praised in the Old Testament: "Do not follow your base desires, but restrain your appetites."[4] In the New Testament it is called "moderation" or "sobriety." We ought "to live sober, upright, and godly lives in this world." [5,6]

Temperance frees us from a joyless obsession and compulsion for the goods of this world. It foments stewardship in managing our God-given gifts for the benefit of ourselves and others. If we are temperate, there is no need for anxiety and worry, which can result from our greed for comforts and large profits. When it comes to worldly wealth, temperance teaches us to recognize when enough is enough.[7]

---

[3] Sir. 5:2, cf. 37:27–31.
[4] Sir. 18:30.
[5] Titus 2:12.
[6] *Catechism of the Catholic Church*, 2nd ed., para. 1809.
[7] Charles Murphy, "The Good Life from a Catholic Perspective: The Problem of Consumption," accessed December. 23, 2017, http://www.usccb.org/sdwp/ejp/articles/goodlife.shtml.

7

Pray, Hope, and Don't Worry

Do not worry about tomorrow;
tomorrow will take care of itself.
—Matthew 6:34

Saint Padre Pio's prescription for eternal health—"Pray, Hope and Don't Worry"—is certainly a fitting message for our time of stress and uncertainty. [1] This motto is the synopsis of his application of theology into daily life. We Christians should recognize God in everything, offering all to Him saying, "Thy will be done." We should aspire to heaven, trust in Him, and not worry about what we are doing, so long as it is done with the intent to please God.

As stated by Father Andrew Apostoli of the Franciscan Friars of the Renewal, "Once you make known your needs, fears, hopes, concerns, doubts, and struggles to God in prayer and have asked for his help, you have to now trust the Lord to listen because of his great compassion." If we worry further about our needs, then doing so may show that we are still trying to control matters that belong to God. Father Apostoli concludes that we should not worry if we really believe that God loves us and will take care of us. He quotes Saint Padre Pio, who said, "The Lord is a father, the most tender and best of fathers. He cannot fail to be moved when his children appeal to him."

---

[1] This chapter draws from the article "Pray, Hope and Don't Worry" by Joseph Pronechen, which appeared on p. B1 of the September 20–26, 2009, issue of the *National Catholic Register*, and from "Pardre Pio the Man—Biography," accessed September 28, 2017, http://www.ewtn.com/padrepio/man/biography2.htm.

This assurance was given to Moses more than three millennia ago when the Lord said to Moses:

> 18 Observe my precepts and be careful to keep my regulations, for then you will dwell securely in the land.
>
> 19 The land will yield its fruit and you will have food in abundance, so that you may live there without worry (Leviticus 25:18–19).

Again, in Luke 12:22-26 Jesus said to his disciples:

> 22 Therefore I tell you, do not worry about your life and what you will eat, or about your body and what you will wear.
>
> 23 For life is more than food and the body more than clothing.
>
> 24 Notice the ravens: they do not sow or reap; they have neither storehouse nor barn, yet God feeds them. How much more important are you than birds!
>
> 25 Can any of you by worrying add a moment to your lifespan?
>
> 26 If even the smallest things are beyond your control, why are you anxious about the rest?

Yes, investing in an uncertain world is often complex and challenging, and it ultimately impacts both our families and others to whom we should lend a helping hand. However, Padre Pio's prescription for eternal health reveals to us that prayer and confidence in God gives us freedom from worry when investing with the intent to serve God through how we touch human life. So "pray, hope, and don't worry." As Saint Paul said in Philippians 4:4–7:

4 Rejoice in the Lord always. I shall say it again: rejoice!

5 Your kindness should be known to all. The Lord is near.

6 Have no anxiety at all, but in everything, by prayer and petition, with thanksgiving, make your requests known to God.

7 Then the peace of God that surpasses all understanding will guard your hearts and minds in Christ Jesus.

PART II

Investing Principles, Facts,
and Guidelines

The Basic Nature of Investing

The concepts of returns and compound interest
are essential to understanding investing.

The basic nature of investing is simple. Investing occurs when you put aside funds with the intent of growing that amount of money for later use. In order to grow money you must earn a profit on it. For example, you might invest $100 in a bank account that pays 10 percent interest, or $10 per year; then at the end of the first year there will be $110 in the account. If you leave the $100 plus the $10 in the bank for a second year then you will have $121, and so on.

For each year, your annual *return* is equal to the money you earn stated as a *percentage* of the size of your investment at the *beginning* of the year. For the first year, you earn $10 on $100 invested; this is a 10 percent return. For year two, you get another $10 for the interest on your original $100, plus $1 interest on the $10 interest you earned in year one. Thus, at the end of year two, the original $100 has earned a total of $10 in year one, plus $10 in year two, plus another $1 in year two, for a total of $21 of interest earned. When interest is earned on interest, this is referred to as *compound interest.*

Other investments work in a similar way. For example, if you buy $100 worth of a stock and the stock rises to $110 in value by the end of year one, then your profit is $10, which equals a return of 10 percent. If at the end of year two your stock is worth $121, your return is again 10 percent based on the $110 value at the beginning of year two. However, if at the end of year one your stock has fallen in value to $90, then your return is a loss of 10 percent. Returns are computed in the same manner for houses, stocks, bonds, or any other investment you make. Now let us turn to the primary types of investments.

The Primary Types of Investments

*The four primary investment vehicles
are bank accounts, stocks, bonds, and real estate.*

The primary types of investments include the following: bank accounts, stocks, bonds, and real estate. Here, we look at each of these and also at the ways you can invest in them.

We are all familiar with *bank accounts*, which are created when we keep money in a bank checking account, savings account, certificate of deposit (CD), or money market account. These usually pay interest and are very safe because, even if the bank fails, checking accounts, savings accounts, and CDs are all insured by the Federal Deposit Insurance Corporation (FDIC). You have ready access to your funds in the bank. However, with CDs, you may incur a small penalty if you need the money on short notice.

Investors should keep several months' worth of expense money in a bank account for unforeseen needs, such as illness or job loss. Bank savings should be only a small portion of one's total investments because of their low returns, as we'll see in chapter 14.

Unlike a bank account, *stock* represents ownership in a company. If a company sells 100,000 shares of stock to the public, and you buy 1,000 shares, you are a 1 percent owner of that company. As an owner of *common* stock, your stock may increase in price if the company prospers over time. You may also receive *dividends*, which are the portions of company profits paid out to stockholders.

If you decide to sell stock, you can usually get your money in a matter of days.

Stock investments should be a significant portion of most investors' portfolios. Stocks have returned more than any other class of investments over the past century and will likely continue to do so over the years to come. The growth in value from stocks can be substantial. Yes, stocks are riskier because, as seen in chapter 14, their returns vary more than the returns of other assets. Over the long run, however, they should allow one to generate greater assets that can be used in the Lord's service.

Bonds are loans made by you to a company that pays you *interest* to use your money. Bonds are sold in $1,000 face amounts and pay interest as a percentage of the face value. A 6 percent bond will pay $60 per year to the bondholder. After a period of time, you, the bondholder, are repaid the face amount ($1,000) for each bond owned. *Maturity* is the amount of time it takes until a bond is paid off at its face value. Bondholders are paid interest before stockholders are paid dividends.

Over the longer term, bonds generally return more than bank savings but less than stocks. The certainty of bond returns that comes from their coupon payments makes them appropriate for cash flow needs, such as living expenses during retirement.

Approximately half of households in the United States own stocks and/or bonds. However, the majority of individuals purchase mutual funds instead of buying stocks or bonds directly.

Mutual funds are special companies formed to raise money by selling shares of their stock and then investing this money in a variety of stocks and bonds. These companies are managed by professionals who are paid a fee for overseeing the portfolio or collection of investments held by the fund. Any profits above the management fee are paid to the shareholders of the mutual fund. As with bank accounts, stocks, and bonds, you can get your money quickly when you sell mutual fund shares.

For many of us, our home constitutes our primary real estate asset. Generally speaking, real estate has been a reasonable investment over long periods of time and will probably continue to be. Historically, many people have benefited financially from owning a home rather than renting. But the drawbacks of ownership include upkeep, taxes, maintenance, etcetera. Even though home ownership represents a significant investment for many people, in this book, we will focus primarily on liquid (easily converted to cash) assets such as bank deposits, stocks, bonds, and mutual funds. In the next chapter, let's look more closely at these different investments.

10

Bank Investing

Banks are safe places to keep money you may need quickly.

When we keep our money in a bank, it goes into a checking account, a savings account, a certificate of deposit (CD), or a money market account. In return for the bank's use of our money, we are paid interest.

The bank states what our interest will be. For example, a savings deposit may pay us 3 percent annually. Thus, the bank will pay us $3 if we keep $100 in the account for one year. Our return is the interest received as a percentage of our deposit.

Checking accounts usually pay the least interest. Savings accounts pay somewhat more. However, if we agree to leave our deposit with the bank for a certain period of time—two years, for example—then the bank will usually pay an even higher rate. The period of time that you agree to deposit your money in a CD generally varies from 30 days up to five years.

Money deposited in checking accounts, savings accounts, and CDs is guaranteed by the Federal Deposit Insurance Corporation up to the amount of $250,000. Then, even if the bank fails, your insured money is safe.

Money market accounts are not insured by the FDIC. Nonetheless, money market accounts invest in short-term bond equivalents and are very safe. They frequently pay a slightly higher return than savings accounts because they are not insured.

Stock Investing

Stocks are used for long-term investing.

Stock represents ownership in a firm and can be bought in small companies or huge companies, like Microsoft. A company's size is measured by its market capitalization (market cap), which equals the total value of all of its stock. For example, Microsoft shareholders own roughly 10 billion shares of stock with a market price of $95. Its market cap is 10 billion multiplied by $95, or $950 billion. Companies with more than $5 billion market cap are called large-cap companies. Small caps are less than $1 billion in size, and mid caps are in the middle.

Now let's look at a stock's rate of return for a single year. Return includes the price gain or loss of a stock, plus any dividends paid. Assume Company ABC's stock was $100 per share on January 1 and closed at $110 on December 31 one year later. Its price increased by $10 per share, or 10 percent ($10 divided by $100 equals 0.1, or 10 percent). If ABC also paid a $3 dividend during the year, then it had a 3 percent dividend return. The stock's total rate of return is 10 percent + 3 percent, or 13 percent for the year.

For investment purposes, a good tool for comparing one company to another is the price-to-earnings (P/E) ratio. Consider two companies: ABC and XYZ.

ABC has 10,000 shares outstanding (owned by shareholders) and earns $20,000 yearly, after all expenses. It earns $2.00 per share ($20,000 divided by 10,000 shares). If the shares sell on the stock market at $24 each, then the P/E ratio is $24/$2, or 12.

XYZ has 1,000,000 shares outstanding and earns $1,000,000 per year. As we see, it earns $1 per share. Since XYZ's shares sell at $50 each, its P/E ratio is $50/$1, or 50.

We see that investors are willing to pay $50 for each $1 of XYZ earnings, compared to $12 for each $1 of ABC earnings. The P/E ratio shows what investors pay for $1 worth of earnings, regardless of a company's size. This allows investors to compare companies across size and industries.

Some investment managers prefer to buy low P/E stocks because their prices tend to be less volatile than the prices of high P/E stocks. *Value stocks* usually have low P/Es like 8, 10, or 15, while *growth stocks* have P/Es like 25, 50, or even more. Over the last 90 years, value stocks have, on average, given investors higher rates of return than have growth stocks.

Bond Investing

Bonds are relatively safe and pay steady income.

As seen in chapter 9, bonds are IOUs issued by either companies or governments to bond investors who lend money to the issuer for a certain period of time. During this time, investors are paid interest by the issuer for the use of their money. At maturity the $1,000 face amount per bond is returned to the investor.

The US government issues short-maturity IOUs called *treasury bills* that mature in one year or less. Their longer-maturing bonds are called *treasury bonds*. Investors pay federal income taxes on the interest from these bills and bonds. US government bonds are the safest bonds and have never failed to pay interest or the $1,000 per-bond face amount of principal to their bondholders at maturity.

States, cities, and counties issue bonds that pay interest that isn't subject to federal income taxes. These are called *municipals* and are almost as safe as US government bonds. However, on rare occasions some cities have been late with interest payments.

Companies issue bonds called *corporates*, which pay interest. The amount of interest the bondholder receives depends on how much interest the company is able to pay. While the interest from these bonds is more than that of treasuries or municipals, corporates may or may not be safe. Safety ratings of bonds range from A+ on down. Bonds with ratings in the A and B+ ranges are considered high quality. *Junk bonds* have B ratings and are not as safe; therefore, their current yields are higher than other bonds.

Let's consider a bond's rate of return for a single year. Return includes the price gain or loss of a bond, plus any interest paid. If Company ABC's bond is $1,000 on January 1, and closes at $1,050 on December 31 of the same year, its price has increased by $50, or 5 percent ($50 divided by $1000 equals 0.05). If ABC also pays $60 interest during the year, then it generates 6 percent interest return. The bond's total rate of return is 5 percent + 6 percent, or 11 percent for the year.

Most bonds are first sold at a price close to their face value ($1,000). When they later trade on the bond market, their price is usually higher or lower than $1,000. This is because market interest rates go up or down. The risk of rates going up or down is called *interest rate risk*. If current interest rates go up, the prices of old bonds (for example, with a 5 percent fixed interest rate) drop because newer bonds pay a higher interest rate (say 6 percent fixed) than old bonds. People sell the old 5 percent bonds to buy the 6 percent bonds because of the better rates. The price of old bonds must fall—that makes sense. However, if an investor holds any bond until it matures, the investor is paid $1,000 by the issuer to retire the bond.

Mutual Funds

Mutual funds are a popular, easy way to diversify.

A *mutual fund* is a company that pools peoples' money and invests this money in stocks or bonds. The fund issues shares of its own stock in exchange for an investor's money. Profits from its investments are paid out to its shareholders.

There are good reasons to buy mutual funds. One reason is to have a professional manager to look after your money. Another reason is that mutual funds keep records of the stocks and bonds they own on your behalf. A third good reason is that you get instant diversification via the fund's different investments.

Mutual funds are easy to purchase. You can buy a mutual fund's shares directly from the fund. Your money goes to the fund; they issue you their stock; and they invest the money on your behalf. Funds that are sold directly to investors are *no-load funds*. These funds are bought or sold without commissions.

Alternately, you can use a broker to buy mutual fund shares. Funds that are handled through brokers or other financial institutions are usually called *load funds*. The seller charges sales fees depending upon the fund and the amount of money you invest.[1]

A mutual fund makes its money by charging a management

---

[1] An exchange-traded fund (ETF) is a relatively recent type of investment portfolio that is traded on the securities exchanges. These are discussed in chapter 31.

fee to invest and keep records. Some charge a small fee like 0.25 percent per year. Others charge much more, like 2 percent per year, or even higher, depending upon the fund.

Do mutual funds make money for their shareholders? Yes, as a rule, both bond funds and stock funds make money for shareholders. Stock mutual funds usually make money because they invest in stocks, and stock prices tend to rise over long periods of time. Bond funds pay their shareholders the interest collected from a portfolio of bonds.

Now let's take a quick look at annuities that are often closely related to mutual funds. Simply put, *annuities* are a given amount of money that you invest, from which you withdraw your principal and earnings over a future period. The two basic types of annuities are fixed annuities and variable annuities. Fixed annuities are investment contracts (usually sold by insurance companies) that pay you a fixed amount for a given period, or for the rest of your life, depending upon the terms of the contract. Variable annuities are contracts where your money is usually invested in mutual funds. These annuities pay you a variable amount of money over time, depending upon their investment returns. Oftentimes, annuities are very complicated and expensive to own.

Historical Returns and Risk

Historical returns are the best estimate of what returns are likely to be over the long-term future.

Here, we consider the *historical* returns and risks of different investment choices. Table 14.1 gives the average annual returns for different asset classes over the period 1926–2016. The particular measure of risk shown in the table is the *volatility* of that class's returns.[1]

Table 14.1
Average Asset Returns and Risk, 1926–2016

Asset	Return percent	Risk percent
Large cap	11	20
Small cap	13	33
Value stocks	13	28
Growth stocks	9	20
Bonds	6	9
Real Estate	5	7
T-bills	3	3
Bank Savings	3	2

---

[1] These numbers are estimates taken from Ibbotson (2016) and from the author's research.

Table 14.1 shows that small company stocks have returned more than large company stocks, and that value stocks have returned more than growth stocks. All categories of stock have higher historical returns and more risk than bonds, real estate, or treasury bills.

Let's put volatility into perspective. As we often hear on the news, the stock market goes up some days and down on others. At the beginning of the Great Depression stocks declined more than 80 percent. Other substantial declines occurred in 1937, 1974, 2000, and 2008. Even so, over time the market has risen at an average annual rate of approximately 12 percent during the past eight decades.

Yes, there have been some extreme down years, but if investors had continued to hold their stocks following these years, it would usually have taken only a few years to regain their losses. This is why stocks are longer-term investments.

Taxes, Inflation, and Real Returns

What you have in real terms is what you use to serve others.

Taxes and inflation are two important factors that should be considered when investment decisions are made. Inflation is a general rise in the cost of goods and services, thereby eating away at the worth of your money. For example, a loaf of bread cost 19¢ in the 1960s. Fifty years later, the same loaf cost more than $2.00. In real terms, you are dealing with buying a loaf of bread. In nominal terms the loaf is a different price in each period, but it is the same real loaf.

The effect of taxes is more easily seen because taxes are paid out as money is earned. Let us assume that you're in the 33 percent tax bracket for each additional dollar of ordinary income (like salary and interest income) that you earn. However, under current tax law that Congress can change, you pay only 15 percent in taxes on capital gains (from selling stock) and many dividends that you earn.

Table 15.1 shows asset class returns from table 14.1, and how taxes and inflation ultimately affect these returns and your wealth. Take a look at the large-cap line. If you have an 11 percent return (gains plus dividends), about 15 percent (or one-sixth) of the 11 percent return will go to taxes. Your after-tax return becomes 9.4 percent. If inflation rises at 3 percent annually, your entire monetary wealth is worth 3 percent less than it was one year ago. So, what you have in real terms relative to where you started is what your wealth becomes in terms of the goods and services you can purchase. After maintaining your principal value, you can buy 6.4 percent more real goods after your 11 percent return than you could have with your principal at the start of the year. Taxes and inflation combined ate up the 4.6 percent difference.

Table 15.1
The Effect of Taxes and Inflation on Returns

Asset class	Return percent	Tax percent	After- tax return percent	Inflation percent	Real wealth return percent
Large cap	11	1.6	9.4	3	6.4
Small cap	13	1.9	11.1	3	8.1
Value stock	13	1.9	11.1	3	8.1
Growth stock	9	1.4	7.6	3	4.6
Long bonds	6	1.8	4.2	3	1.2
Real estate	5	1.5	3.5	3	0.5
T-bills	3	0.9	2.1	3	-0.9
Bank savings	3	0.9	2.1	3	-0.9

Looking down the right-hand column, you see that small-cap and value stocks give you the best real return of about 8 percent. The worst you can expect occurs when you buy treasury bills or when you put your money into banks. After taxes and inflation, you actually lose money. Some people counter with "Yes, but money in the bank is safe." To a degree, this is correct. However, inflation and taxes still eat away at what the money can actually buy. Hence, most of us need to invest in stocks if we are going to protect the real value of our money. It should be noted that since 1926, inflation has risen at an annual rate of 3 percent. To put this seemingly small rate in perspective, we can look at the price of an item that cost $1 at that time. To buy the same thing now, you would have to pay $12. This helps explain why people need to grow their savings over time and not simply put it under a rock for safety's sake.

Let us consider the approximate amount of nominal dollars that a retired person will need in order to maintain a real $40,000 annual expenditure over a 30-year period. The nominal figures in table 15.2 assume an annual inflation rate of 3 percent.

Table 15.2
Annual Inflated Expenditures

Year	Amount
2018	$40,000
2023	$46,000
2028	$54,000
2033	$62,000
2038	$84,000
2043	$97,000
2048	$112,000

To generate $40,000 in spendable, real income annually, many investment advisors assume that you begin with $1 million. This is because a typical portfolio with a blend of safety, income, and growth investments has historically returned approximately 7 percent, or $70,000 annually. If so, then one can draw down 4 percent ($40,000 in this case) and reinvest the other $30,000. This 3 percent reinvestment rate will grow the portfolio enough for you to be able to increase your annual, spendable income at a rate equal to the 3 percent rate of inflation. Hence, in the future, you will have a real spendable income equal to $40,000 in today's money. It is the real value or purchasing power of our money that allows us to serve the Lord with our material blessings.

Expenses and Portfolio Value

Expenses can greatly reduce your returns.

The two prior chapters show the impact of taxes and inflation on investor returns and worth. Here, we consider how *expenses* reduce the returns to your portfolio.

Investment expenses come in two forms: (1) commissions (sales fees) that are usually paid when investments are bought or sold, and (2) annual fees charged by investment managers. These fees and commissions are charged throughout the investment industry and can amount to significant sums when viewed in relation to the annual returns generated by different investments.

For example, commissions that are often charged by major investment houses can be 1 to 2 or more percent of the value of a single buy-or-sell transaction. Although 1 to 2 percent does not initially appear to be very much, it must be considered in light of annual returns, as seen in table 16.1. One must also note that the more frequently one trades securities, the higher the expenses become.

Annual fees are the other primary source of expense. Some investment professionals charge an annual fee of 1 to 3 percent to manage investment accounts. Also, different mutual funds (and ETFs as well) charge differing amounts for fees, as we will discuss in the following chapter. Again, 1 to 3 percent does not initially seem to be a large amount, but let's consider the impact of these amounts on the real returns generated by different investment classes, as seen in the prior chapter.

In table 16.1, the second column lists the annual real returns (returns adjusted for inflation and taxes) taken from chapter 15. Columns 3 and 4 show the impact of 1 percent annual expense. The same is done in columns 5 and 6 for 3 percent expense.

Table 16.1
The Effect of Expenses on Real Returns

Asset class	Real return percent	1 percent expense	After 1 percent expense return	3 percent expense	After 3 percent expense return
Large cap	6.4	1	5.4	3	3.4
Small cap	8.1	1	7.1	3	5.1
Value stock	8.1	1	7.1	3	5.1
Growth stock	4.6	1	3.6	3	1.6
Long bonds	1.2	1	0.2	3	-1.8
Real estate	0.5	1	-0.5	3	-2.5
T-bills	-0.9	*	-0.9	*	-0.9
Bank savings[1]	-0.9	*	-0.9	*	-0.9

As seen in column 4, the impact of a 1 percent annual expense is substantial when compared to the historical returns of all investments, especially the lower-risk ones such as bonds and treasury bills. However, when a 3 percent annual expense is considered, the returns for these same investments actually go negative. The impact of expenses can obviously be devastating on returns. In the next chapter we consider expenses from a different perspective.

---

[1] The asterisks indicate that bank savings and T-bills are sometimes not subject to fees charged by managers.

Expenses and Future Portfolio Value

Expenses can greatly reduce future portfolio worth.

In the prior chapter, we considered the effect of expenses on returns. The purpose of this chapter is to emphasize the effect that expenses have on future portfolio value.

Assume you invest $10,000 in a hypothetical mutual fund with no fees, expenses, or taxes for 15 years. If the fund returns 8 percent annually, then your portfolio's ending value will be roughly $31,700. Your profit will be $21,700 ($31,700 minus your $10,000 principal).

Now look at what you might have foregone or lost to different levels of expenses over time. Column 3 in table 17.1 shows the final profits you would make after you pay 3.0 percent, 2.0 percent. 1.0 percent or 0.3 percent expenses each year.[1] Column 4 shows what the fees and expenses keep you from earning over the 15-year period.

If you pay 3.0 percent in yearly expenses, the 8 percent annual return becomes only 5 percent. If you compound $10,000 at 8 percent for 15 years, you end with $31,700. If you compound $10,000 at 5 percent for 15 years you have $20,800. The difference of $10,900 is how much you did not make because of the 3 percent expenses.

---

[1] The range of annual expenses encompasses what the author believes to be representative of how much the vast majority of investors pay annually. This belief is based on work in the investments industry and service as an expert witness in this area.

Consider the bottom line of the table. It shows the long-term impact of a 0.3 percent expense, which is the amount charged by some passively managed funds (these are discussed further in a later chapter). These funds simply buy a small amount of each security on the market. With such an index fund, you would have made $20,400, with only $1,300 lost to expenses.

Table 17.1
Investor Profits and Lost Profits

Nominal return	Annual expenses	Investor profits	Lost to expenses
8.0 percent	3.0 percent	$10,800	$10,900
8.0 percent	2.0 percent	$14,000	$7,700
8.0 percent	1.0 percent	$17,600	$4,100
8.0 percent	0.3 percent	$20,400	$1,300

Thus, at first, 2 percent or 3 percent may not seem to be a significant amount to pay in expenses. However, upon closer examination, these amounts strongly impact the returns you get from investing and thereby have a substantial effect on the monies available for the future good you can do.

The Pros and Cons of Using Investment Advisors

Advisors may be helpful or only an unnecessary expense.

Investment advisors can be very useful for people who need financial guidance. However, they may be an unnecessary expense for those who are comfortable with their own investing abilities. Should you use the services of an investment advisor? This is a question you must answer for yourself. Perhaps a little general information may be helpful with this matter.

Several decades ago, anyone who wished to invest in securities had to use an account representative with a national retail brokerage house, such as Merrill Lynch, or a regional or local house. However, over the past 40 years, the financial services industry has evolved in many ways. Today one may choose from a traditional retail brokerage house, or from a variety of discount brokerages and online services.

Obviously, these organizations charge fees or commissions for their services, and these expenses vary widely. If one utilizes an online business or a discount broker such as Charles Schwab or Vanguard, the commissions to buy or sell securities may amount to only a few dollars per transaction. This results in only a small fraction of 1 percent in cost for each trade. In contrast, when using a full-service house, the same trade may cost $100 or more, which can equal 1 to 2 percent of the transaction.

In a different vein, some financial advisors allow investors the option of paying a fixed percent of their assets annually for their services. Such accounts are often referred to as *wrap accounts* or *managed accounts*, and the fees often range from 2 to 3 percent annually.

Regardless of which alternative you choose, you should keep in mind the prior discussion of expenses from chapters 16 and 17, which show that it is prudent to minimize expenses because of their impact on returns and future portfolio value. It is essential to interview either in person or via telephone both discount brokers and full-service houses to learn about their services and their fees and commissions. Do not be bashful. These are God's assets entrusted to you that you are managing in his service.

To Do and Not to Do

Here are some general guidelines for prudent investing.

When investing, it is best to take a long-term view. Successful investors are those who have well-defined, reasonable goals and who exercise patience in seeking to attain them. They are not gamblers who frequently trade securities for short-term gain and who usually fritter away their assets via trading expenses. Nor do they attempt to jump into or out of the market based on short-term fear and hope.

Those who seek success in these ways are usually doomed to failure, and this is nothing new. I am aware of many people who have speculated with disastrous results over the past several decades, especially during the early 1970, the late 1990s, and the 2008 stock market meltdown. Much further back, one can find many references of market gaming and speculation, as exemplified by comments in the May 1853 issue of *Hunt's Merchants' Magazine* concerning many people of modest means who lost their life savings gambling in the securities market.[1]

Successful investing, on the other hand, involves making rational decisions and being well diversified. One must not allocate too large a portion of a portfolio to safety because of the low returns generated by bank accounts and short-term bonds. Nor should one employ a disproportionate amount of income-oriented securities,

---

[1] Referenced in Krooss and Blyn, 68.

especially during one's prime working years. During early- and mid-life, stocks should play a predominant role in portfolios because of their long-term growth potential, which is necessary to offset the effects of inflation. In later life one should usually move more toward securities characterized by income and safety.

PART III

Morally Responsible Investing

The US Bishops' Position on Morally Responsible Investing

We are called to follow Jesus in our economic endeavors.

The US Catholic Bishops' basic position on morally responsible investing is put forth in the first paragraph of the pastoral letter *Economic Justice for All*, wherein the bishops write:

> Brothers and Sisters in Christ:
>
> 1. We are believers called to follow Our Lord Jesus Christ and proclaim his Gospel in the midst of a complex and powerful economy ... Economic decisions have human consequences and moral content; they help or hurt people, strengthen or weaken family life, advance or diminish the quality of justice in our land.

They then draw paragraph 5 from the *Pastoral Constitution on the Church in the Modern World*, No. 43, which states:

> 5. Followers of Christ must avoid a tragic separation between faith and everyday life. They can neither shirk their earthly duties nor, as the Second Vatican Council declared, "immerse [them]selves in earthly

activities as if these latter were utterly foreign to religion ..."

Insofar as the above paragraphs pertain to investing per se, the bishops continue in paragraph 354:

354. Individual Christians who are shareholders and those responsible within church institutions that own stocks in U.S. corporations must see to it that the invested funds are used responsibly ... As part owners, they must cooperate in shaping the policies of those companies through dialogue with management, [etc.] ... which help the Church respond to local and regional needs. When the decision to divest seems unavoidable, it should be done after prudent examination and with a clear explanation of the motives.

Although paragraph 354 delineates the fiduciary responsibilities in Christian investing, the specific guidelines for investment endeavors are discussed by the bishops in Socially Responsible Investment Guidelines. These guidelines are the subject of the following chapters.

Two Principles of Investment Stewardship

We are to seek reasonable returns
while adhering to Catholic moral teachings.

The Socially Responsible Investment Guidelines issued by the USCCB address the two fundamental principles of stewardship pertaining to the Conference's management of financial resources: obtaining a reasonable market-based rate of return on investments and implementing investment strategies based on Catholic moral teachings. According to the bishops, "these two major principles ... are carried out through strategies that seek: 1) to avoid participation in harmful activities, 2) to use the Conference's role as stockholder for social stewardship, and 3) to promote the common good."[1]

These three strategies are delineated as:

1. *Do no harm.* ... This strategy involves two ... courses of action: 1) refusal to invest in companies whose ... policies are counter to the values of Catholic moral teaching; 2) divesting from such companies ...

2. *Active Corporate Participation.* Given the ... teaching of *Economic Justice for All*, it seems appropriate for the Conference to adopt a strategy of active ... participation with regard to its stock holdings in accord with Conference policies.

---

[1] Socially Responsible Investment Guidelines, section 3.

3. *Positive Strategies.* ... These strategies involve ... two possible courses of action: 1) supporting policies and initiatives in companies owned by the Conference that promote the values of Catholic moral ... teaching ... while earning a reasonable rate of return; 2) investments that promote community development. ...

How to implement these strategies is the subject of the USCCB investment policies. We now turn to these.

USCCB Investment Policies

The United States Conference of Catholic Bishops' investment policies cover the following areas: protecting human life, promoting human dignity, reducing arms production, pursuing economic justice, protecting the environment, and encouraging corporate responsibility. In their Socially Responsible Investment Guidelines, they lay forth their respective policies:[1]

I. Protecting Human Life

Human life is sacred because from its beginning it involves 'the creative action of God' ... who ... alone is the Lord of life from its beginning until its end. ...

Abortion—"... we proclaim that human life is a precious gift from God ... and that society ... must protect and nurture human life at every stage ..."

Policy—In view of the nature of abortion, the investment policy of the USCCB should remain as it is, namely, *absolute exclusion* of investment in companies whose activities include direct ... support of abortion.

---

[1] In the interest of brevity, neither the entire text nor its sources are quoted. The reader can access the full text at http://www.usccb.org/about/financial-reporting/socially-responsible-investment-guidelines.cfm.

Contraceptives—"The Church ... teaches that ... every marital act must of necessity retain its intrinsic relationship to the procreation of human life."

Policy—In view of the Church's clear teaching ... the USCCB will not invest in companies that manufacture contraceptives or derive a significant portion of its revenues from the sale of contraceptives. ...

Embryonic Stem Cell / Human Cloning—"No objective ... can ... justify experimentation on living human embryos or fetuses, whether viable or not, either inside or outside the mother's womb ..."

Policy—The USCCB will not invest in companies that engage in scientific research on human fetuses or embryos that (1) results in the end of pre-natal human life; (2) makes use of tissue derived from ... life-ending activities; or (3) violates the dignity of a developing person.

II. Promoting Human Dignity

Human Rights—"Promotion of the full complement of human rights and religious liberty ... remains a central priority for our conference ..."

Policy—USCCB will actively promote and support shareholder resolutions directed towards ... promoting human rights.

Racial Discrimination—"Discrimination based on the accidental fact of race or color ... cannot be reconciled with the truth that God has created all men with equal rights and ... dignity."

Policy—USCCB will divest from ... companies ... found to be discriminatory against people of varied ethnic and racial backgrounds. ...

Gender Discrimination—"Since women are becoming ever more conscious of their human dignity, they will not tolerate being treated as mere material instruments. ..."

Policy—The USCCB will divest from those companies whose policies are found to be discriminatory against women.

Access to Pharmaceuticals (e.g., HIV/AIDS)— "Most [Africans] lack access to health services or safe drinking water. ..."

Policy—USCCB will encourage companies to undertake or participate in programs designed to make life-sustaining drugs available to those in low-income communities and countries at reduced, affordable prices.

Curbing Pornography—"Pornography itself ... denies the dignity which God gives each human being ..."

Policy—The USCCB will not invest in a company that derives a significant portion of its revenues from products ... intended exclusively to appeal to a prurient interest in sex. ...

III. Reducing Arms Production

Production and Sale of Weapons—"While extravagant sums are being spent for the furnishing of ever new weapons ... Disagreements between nations are not ... healed."

Policy—The Conference ... seeks to discourage any nuclear and conventional arms race. ...

Antipersonnel   Landmines—"Government controls do not absolve those involved in the arms industry of moral responsibility for their decisions to sell arms."

Policy—USCCB will not invest in companies that are directly involved in ... anti-personnel landmines.

IV. Pursuing Economic Justice

Labor Standards / Sweatshops—"If the dignity of work is to be protected, then the basic rights of workers must be respected. ..."

Policy—USCCB will actively promote and support shareholder resolutions directed towards avoiding ... sweatshops in the manufacture of goods.

Affordable Housing / Banking—"We must insure fair and equal access to available credit. ..."

Policy—The Conference will not deposit funds in a financial institution that receives less than a "satisfactory" rating from federal regulatory agencies. ...

V. Protecting the Environment

"Our tradition calls us to protect the life and dignity of the human person, and it is increasingly clear that this task cannot be separated from the care and defense of all creation. ..."

Policy—USCCB investment policy will actively promote and support shareholder resolutions which encourage corporations to act "to preserve the planet's ecological heritage, [etc.] ..."

VI. Encouraging Corporate Responsibility—"The private sector must be not only an engine of growth and productivity, but also a reflection of our values and priorities, a contributor to the common good. Examples of greed and misconduct must be replaced with models of corporate responsibility."

Policy—USCCB will encourage companies to report on social, environmental, as well as financial performance.

Moral Investing Challenges for Individuals

*It is often difficult to determine the
moral desirability of investing in an enterprise.*

In the prior three chapters, we visited the USCCB position on socially responsible investing, as laid out in *Economic Justice for All* and Socially Responsible Investment Guidelines. The bishops call for both the Conference and individual Christian investors to "exercise faithful, competent and socially responsible stewardship"[1] in the management of financial resources.

The two fundamental principles of stewardship are: (1) to obtain a reasonable market-based rate of return on investments, and (2) to implement investment strategies based on the moral demands "posed by the virtues of prudence and justice."[2] A reasonable rate of return is relatively easy to estimate and quantify, depending upon the type of investment involved, as seen in chapter 14. However, as to the second principle, even with the financial resources and advisors available to the Church, it is no small task for its investment stewards to readily determine the moral desirability of investing in any given firm. This is often due to the lack of transparency concerning the company's activities as well as the evolution of its products and services over time.

For *individual* investors with more limited resources and expertise, this second principle of stewardship is likely even more difficult to implement than it is for the Church's investment

---

[1] SRIG, 1.
[2] SRIG, 2.

stewards. Some firms may easily be excluded from consideration because of obviously immoral products or policies that violate a specific moral principle addressed by the Conference. However, the suitability of other firms may be more difficult to determine because of their sheer size and their varied worldwide activities.

In a kindred vein, individual investors oftentimes do not know what is included in their investment accounts, pension accounts, or annuities, which are managed by institutional investors. For example, the author has a 403-b plan established by his employer. It is effectively impossible to keep up with the investment holdings of the various accounts employed. Such is the case for many investors who utilize any of a variety of retirement accounts. After all, most people are too busy with their work, or have little interest or expertise in investigating all of the firms such plans hold.

What is one to do in such a situation? Money should not simply be buried, as did the poor steward in Matthew 25. Christ expects us to be good stewards of our gifts. How to address the various situations we as individuals might encounter is the subject of this chapter.

In *Difficult Moral Questions*, professor of Christian ethics Germain Grisez addresses the following questions asked by an investor nearing retirement:

> May one invest in businesses that supply various good products or services but also supply some things one considers seriously immoral to use? The answer seems clear: Don't do it. But when investing in a mutual fund holding stock in scores of companies, what responsibility does an individual investor have to try to track down all the products or services of all those companies?[3]

Professor Grisez begins by asking whether one should invest for one's own needs and those of dependents, or whether the money

---

[3] Grisez, 502.

should be used to help others in need. If one decides that investing is necessary, he emphasizes that one should invest prudently and not take undue risks for the pure sake of high returns.

When it comes to investing in individual securities, the professor continues by explaining that it is preferable to invest in ventures promoting genuine human needs. As well, he states that companies that promote primarily the interests of their owners and high-level managers, while treating others only as required by contracts and laws, should be avoided:

> For example, a company distributes wholesome foods, advertises unobjectionably, and so on, but exploits its agricultural workers with low pay, no benefits, and wretched working conditions ... or an insurance company, morally above reproach in most respects, deliberately trains its sales agents to deceive potential buyers about their need for insurance and cost-effective ways of meeting that need with a view to maximizing profit for the company and commissions to agents.[4]

However, as discussed in the prior chapter, the task of evaluating the moral desirability of a large company's products and services can be extremely difficult. The building of a portfolio of acceptable firms is likewise challenging. Which firms are to be selected in which industries? How many different securities are required for diversification purposes? Addressing these issue can be burdensome and time-consuming. This brings us to the matter of mutual fund investing, which offers a solution to the problem of portfolio construction and diversification because funds hold a large number of different securities.[5]

---

[4] Grisez, 505.

[5] For reasons of risk and liquidity, it is this author's opinion that most individuals should invest in multiple public market securities or mutual funds rather than in a single public-market or private enterprise.

Addressing the problem of not being able to determine the moral suitability of each fund holding and the problem of monitoring a fund's numerous holdings over time, Professor Grisez provides clear direction, stating:

> You should use any information you have or can easily obtain to steer clear of mutual funds whose holdings seem especially heavy in seriously tainted industries or firms. Therefore, you may invest in a particular mutual fund or funds only if: (a) you have made a reasonable effort to investigate various mutual funds, and (b) you have excluded from consideration any whose policies seem especially likely to lead to the selection of the stocks of businesses that profit from wrongdoing. Certain mutual funds call themselves "socially responsible" and the like, suggesting that their managers use moral criteria in selecting stocks, but the criteria often are secularist rather than Christian. Do not trust such labels unless your study of the criteria, as stated in the fund's prospectus, makes it clear these correspond to sound morality, including the church's social teaching.

We will further pursue the mutual fund topic in chapters 29 and 30. For now, we turn to the impact that investing in stocks or mutual funds has on the particular companies in which we invest.[6]

---

[6] Many other fine points are made in Professor Grisez's "Question 112: May one invest in morally tainted businesses?" The reader is encouraged to refer to the original work for more details on this valuable treatment of such an important issue.

How Your Investment Affects a Company

What happens with your money when you make an investment?

Investing in a business ultimately takes one of two paths: (1) that of an owner, or (2) that of a creditor. Owners are issued stock, and may receive dividends if the company thrives. Creditors essentially make loans and are issued certificates, notes, or bonds. They receive interest for the use of their money and eventually are paid back the loan. In both cases, the investors' money is used in one way or another to promote the business's purpose.

That said, how and when one makes an investment does determine the *impact* of the investment on a particular company. For example, a $10,000 investment in a local venture directly flows to the enterprise regardless of whether it is a stock investment or a loan. The situation is the same if the $10,000 is invested directly in new stock or bonds issued by a large national firm.

In contrast, if the same money is invested in the stock or bond of a company that is traded on the market, then the situation differs because securities that trade on the market after their first issuance are in effect "used" securities. The money paid for them goes to the investor from whom they are purchased, not directly to the company.

When you invest in a typical mutual fund, your money goes into the fund and then the fund purchases securities that trade on the market. The money does not go directly to the company whose shares the fund buys.

Thus, when you invest via stocks or bonds directly in a company, you are providing lifeblood to the enterprise. However, if you buy market-traded securities, whether off the securities exchange or indirectly via a mutual fund, the impact of your actions are negligible on the enterprise. Even though negligible, you are providing price support to the firm's securities, and this ultimately facilitates the ability of the company to raise future funds for its purposes.

This brings us to Professor Grisez's position that:

> Those who directly invest in a company normally intend it to do efficiently all they are aware of its doing to make its profits. If some of the company's profit-enhancing policies and actions are immoral, the investor normally intends the immorality and so shares moral responsibility for it.[1]

The above paragraphs also underlie his position that:

> Just as one can buy certificates of deposit from banks that lend money to all sorts of people and businesses, some of which use the borrowed funds immorally, so one can invest in a mutual equity fund in order to profit from the presumably morally clean operations of diverse businesses represented in the funds, and not intend to gain, but only accept, the tainted profits accruing from businesses that provide bad goods and services.[2]

Yes, how and when you make an investment determines the impact of that investment on a particular company. Direct investing in a company provides its lifeblood, whereas buying used

---

[1] Grisez, 505.
[2] Grisez, 505.

PART IV

Addressing Our Catholic
Investment Responsibilities

Applying Faith-Related Matters to Investing

How can we invest without blindly following worldly practices?

Throughout the world, many are concerned with having enough food to eat, as opposed to having worldly wealth to invest. You, dear reader, and I, should both give thanks to God for our abundant earthly blessings. As well, we must be good stewards in managing the resources entrusted to us for his service.

As seen earlier, according to the USCCB Socially Responsible Investment Guidelines, the two principles of stewardship pertaining to the management of financial resources are: "(1) obtaining a reasonable market-based rate of return ... and (2) implementing investing strategies based on Catholic moral teachings." In seeking to obtain a reasonable rate of return, we should exercise prudence in developing an appropriate portfolio for our time horizon and objectives.

In order to effect temperance in investing, we should strive for order and balance with a diversified portfolio directed toward safety, income, or growth, as needed. Once we understand what are reasonable returns to expect for a given objective, then we are less likely to become anxious about our portfolio's performance. This allows us to ignore the "get rich quick" greed-driven strategies often promoted by some in the investments industry. Thus, we can avoid the worry and disappointment that usually accompanies such avarice.

Some people decide to invest on their own behalf while others choose the services of a financial professional. Regardless of your decision, you must then select individual securities, mutual funds, or some combination of these. When doing so, depending upon your situation as discussed in chapter 23, you may have the opportunity to implement investing strategies in accord with Catholic moral teachings.

Once you develop a portfolio, prudence also requires that you consider the real possibility of your not being able to manage these assets for the entirety of your life, hence the need for another capable person or organization to do so. Additionally, you must plan for the management of and the eventual disposal of your assets after death.

Obviously, each of the above decisions can be daunting. Taken together, they present a time-consuming challenge. However, Saint Padre Pio's motto—"Pray, hope, and don't worry"—reinforces for us that prayer and confidence in God can give us freedom from worry when making these decisions with the intent to please the Lord.

Your Basic Investment Objectives

How you seek a reasonable rate of return depends upon your objectives.

As discussed earlier, the three basic investment *objectives* for most investors are safety, income, and growth, which also correspond to the three basic types of investment vehicles available. Here, we briefly consider these objectives, the types of investments used to achieve them, and the different risk/return characteristics of each category.

The first step is to determine what percentage of your assets should be allocated to which category. A widely used rule of thumb by many financial advisors is to allocate your age percentage to income and safety, and the remainder to growth securities. This is a reasonable guideline to use.

For example, if you are 50 years of age, your initial mix of securities might be 10 percent safety, 40 percent income, and 50 percent growth. Thus, 50 percent should be allocated to stocks, 40 percent to bonds, and 10 percent to CDs or short-term bonds. In contrast, a young adult might have an initial mix of 80 percent growth, 15 percent income, and 5 percent safety.

Safety is appropriate for investors who will need their savings in the near future. The safest investments are bank deposits, such as CDs or savings accounts, and various short-term bonds, which include those issued by high-quality corporations and local, state, or federal governments. As seen in table 26.1, adapted from chapter 14, less risky vehicles give significantly smaller returns than do long-term bonds or stocks.

Investors who need current income are well served by longer-term bonds, high-dividend stocks, or annuities.[1] Longer-term bonds and high-dividend value stocks usually generate higher income than do savings accounts or CDs. However, they are more volatile in price, as indicated by their risk measures.

Growth is the third of the three broad investor objectives. People investing for retirement or other long-term (seven years or more) goals should consider stocks for a relatively larger portion of their assets. As the following table shows, stocks have returned more historically, but also have exhibited more volatility or risk than have bonds or other less-risky securities.

Table 26.1
Average Asset Returns and Risk, 1926–2016

Asset	Return percent	Risk percent
Large cap	11	20
Small cap	13	33
Value stocks	13	28
Growth stocks	9	20
Bonds	6	9
Real estate	5	7
T-bills	3	3
Bank savings	3	2

Thus, you should expect to sacrifice the higher returns given by stocks and bonds if you need the safety and liquidity provided by a bank account or short-term bonds. However, for most investors, care must be taken not to be overly conservative by allocating too much to safety. This is because doing so may make it necessary to

---

[1] Annuities are financial income products managed by life insurance companies. For a discussion of these, please see *Getting Started in Annuities* by Gordon Williamson.

draw down capital to meet current expenses, thereby jeopardizing the assets and the long-term health of the portfolio. Hence, we should exercise prudence in developing a well-balanced portfolio for our time horizon and objectives.

Diversification

Diversification is perhaps the most important aspect of investing.

Diversification is well described by the old saying "Don't put all of your eggs in one basket." An even older saying comes from Ecclesiastes 11:2, which states, "Make seven or eight portions: you know not what misfortune may come upon the earth." This verse refers to the wisdom of not putting all of one's cargo into a single vessel.[1] Likewise, prudent investing requires that one's financial assets be allocated among different investment vehicles.

Early in my life, I learned about diversification from a great-aunt of mine. Aunt Em was a frugal but generous schoolteacher who had her savings in various stocks, bonds, and savings accounts. On occasion she shared her memories of people losing all they had during the stock market turbulence and bank closings of the early 1900s. Her good example of diversifying impressed on me the wisdom of limiting the proportion in each investment to only a small percent of a portfolio.

There are several different benefits from having a diversified portfolio. First, the impact of any given holding's poor performance on your financial health is minimal. Second, greed is less likely to color your perspective because of the relatively small importance of any particular security's return to your total portfolio. Finally, the lower volatility of a diversified portfolio is less likely to cause anxiety.

---

[1] Ecclesiastes 11:2.

When you allocate varying proportions of your portfolio to safety, income, and growth, you have made your initial diversification decision. You may further diversify by dividing your safety funds between bank accounts and money market funds. Your income and growth portions should go to multiple individual bonds or stocks. Alternately, you may employ bond and stock mutual funds for these purposes.

Selecting Individual Securities

Selecting individual securities is no small challenge.

The process of selecting individual securities can require considerable effort and is the topic of thousands of books. For this reason, readers who wish to consider only mutual funds may wish to go directly to the next chapter. This is what I recommend for most people.

In building your portfolio, whether individual securities or mutual funds, you must first determine your primary and secondary objectives as discussed in the prior chapter. Investors in later life usually focus on income and safety, with growth as a secondary objective. Younger investors should focus on growth, with income and safety as secondary objectives. Regardless, you should first determine your primary goal and start from there.

Investing for safety is the easiest decision to make. A bank is the obvious solution because the money is insured up to $250,000 if it is in a savings account or a certificate of deposit. Alternatively, one may purchase a money market fund or US Treasury bills. These are available through discount brokers, full-service brokers, and banks. Diversification is not usually an issue with these holdings.

When it comes to individual securities for income and growth purposes, the challenge becomes much greater and is beyond the scope of this book. There are thousands of books available on the topic of investing. One book that has stood the test of time and that I highly recommend is *The Intelligent Investor*, written by

Benjamin Graham in 1949. This work emphasizes value investing and how such an approach works for investors over the long term.

Once you are comfortable with investing in individual securities and understand which securities meet your investment needs, you must determine which ones meet the USCCB investment guidelines. These goals ultimately promote: "(I) protecting human life; (II) promoting human dignity; (III) reducing arms production; (IV) pursuing economic justice; (V) protecting the environment; and (VI) encouraging corporate responsibility."[1]

Obviously, based on the above, one would exclude purchasing the securities of firms that fail to protect human life, as well as those other companies failing to pass muster in the remaining areas. As to some firms that fail to protect human life, the pro-life organization Life Decisions International publishes *The Boycott List*, which names the companies that provide support to Planned Parenthood.

However, as discussed earlier, it is more difficult to evaluate the moral desirability of many firms' products and services in other areas. Nonetheless, many companies operate in industries that lend themselves toward products and services that are consistent with USCCB guidelines. Examples of these industries are real estate firms, business development companies, public utilities, telecommunications, electronics, energy, and others. Even still, the investor considering these industries has the challenge of determining whether particular companies adhere to basic USCCB guidelines.

---

[1] SRIG, 4.

A Closer Look at Mutual Funds

Here are some important details about mutual funds.

As we discussed in chapter 13, mutual funds are pools of money formed when investors purchase funds' shares. This pool of money is used to buy a portfolio of stocks or bonds, and the profits and income are passed back to the fund shareholders.

Investors can purchase no-load shares directly from some funds and pay no sales commissions. Alternatively, load funds can be bought from brokers who charge commissions of up to roughly 5 percent of the investment amount. These commissions may be paid up front when purchasing Class A shares, or they can be paid over time with other class shares.

Regardless of whether you select load or no-load funds, the managers of these funds are paid yearly fees for their work. The fees are paid to cover the expenses generated by the fund, which include record keeping and portfolio management. Annual fees range from approximately 0.1 percent to 3 percent of assets, depending upon the portfolio managers' activities.

Management takes one of two forms: active or passive. With an actively managed portfolio, securities are chosen depending upon the managers' assessment of how well each security will perform. For example, a manager might choose 50 different stocks, each of which is anticipated to generate above-average returns. This is obviously a difficult task and becomes even more difficult as the fund becomes larger, whereby even more securities must be evaluated and selected. Actively managed funds charge annual fees ranging from 0.75 percent to approximately 3 percent.

In contrast, passive managers simply purchase representative securities of a particular security index. For example, a portfolio manager might mimic the Dow Jones Industrial Average (DJIA) by purchasing shares of each of the 30 stocks comprising the DJIA. The performance of this indexed portfolio will mirror the returns of the DJIA. Passive funds generally charge management fees of 0.5 percent or less.

Another popular mutual fund–type portfolio is the exchange-traded fund (ETF). The shares of ETFs are bought and sold on the stock exchange in the same way as other stocks. The commissions you pay are the same you would pay for other stocks, depending upon the brokerage house you use. Some of these funds charge annual management fees similar to those of index funds.

Each mutual fund has a stated investment objective, which generally corresponds to one or more of the three basic objectives discussed in chapter 26: safety, income, or growth. Funds with a primary objective of safety invest in treasury bills, bank guarantees (banker's acceptances), or short-term bonds issued by high-quality companies. Money market funds and short-term bond funds are such examples.

Income funds typically invest in longer-term bonds issued by governments or corporations. These funds pay higher interest than do money market funds but entail more risk. The specific securities in which a particular fund can invest range from government securities to high-quality corporates to junk bonds issued by troubled firms.

Equity funds invest almost exclusively in stocks. Some of these funds invest in small company stocks and others in very large companies, while others might index to the overall stock market.

As seen in earlier chapters, the particular type of fund one prefers is a function of an investor's objectives. However, with most funds, an investor will necessarily own, albeit indirectly, some securities involved in activities that directly conflict with Church teachings. In the next chapter we turn to a brief presentation of Catholic-oriented mutual funds for those who would prefer to comply more closely with the USCCB Socially Responsible Investment Guidelines.

Catholic-Oriented Mutual Funds

There are several Catholic-oriented mutual funds to choose from.

In this chapter, we look at Catholic-oriented mutual funds. As explained in the prior chapter, index funds and most ETFs build portfolios that mimic a particular segment of securities. For the vast majority of actively managed funds, investment choices are usually based solely on anticipated returns. Because of their decision criteria, most funds are likely to hold the securities of companies that clearly violate Catholic moral teachings. For example, many funds have holdings in drug companies that violate the pro-life position of the Church.

Fortunately, for those who want to invest more closely in keeping with Church teachings, there are several mutual fund families that focus on securities meeting the guidelines set forth by the USCCB.[1] The four most popular groups of Catholic-oriented mutual funds are: (1) Ave Maria Mutual Funds, (2) Epiphany Funds, (3) LKCM Aquinas Funds, and (4) the Timothy Plan. This chapter presents an overview of these fund groups. In table 30.1, each fund is listed with its symbol, total assets, Morningstar ranking, and category of securities held. The Morningstar ranking shows how a particular fund has performed relative to similar funds, with five stars being the best.

---

[1] There are also some financial advisors, such as Thomas Strohbar, who operate within the same context. As far as this author is aware, there is no central organization for these advisors, but several can be located on the internet.

Ave Maria Mutual Funds is the largest family of Catholic mutual funds, with total assets of approximately $2 billion. It has five different no-load funds. The five primary funds and some descriptive information on each one are seen in table 30.1.

Table 30.1
Ave Maria Mutual Funds

Name	Symbol	Holdings	Assets	Begun	Ranking
Growth	AVEGX	Stocks	$580 million	2003	*****
Value	AVEMX	Stocks	$252 million	2006	**
Rising Dividend	AVEDX	Stocks	$861 million	2005	****
World Equity	AVEWX	Stocks	$63 million	2010	**
Bond	AVEFX	Bonds	$316 million	2003	***

Epiphany Funds is a family of two different funds with total assets of approximately $37 million, as seen in table 30.2.

Table 30.2
Epiphany Funds

Name	Symbol	Holdings	Assets	Begun	Ranking
FFV Fund	EPVCX	Stocks	$17 million	2008	**
Income Fund	EPIAX	Bonds	$19 million	2010	****

LKCM Aquinas Fund comprises six different funds, with total assets of approximately $1 billion. These no-load funds are seen in table 30.3.

Table 30.3
LKCM Aquinas Funds

Name	Symbol	Holdings	Assets	Begun	Ranking
Catholic Equity	AQEIX	Stocks	$61 million	2005	**
Balanced Fund	LKBAX	Stocks/bonds	$90 million	1997	****

Equity	LKEQX	Stocks	$365 million	1996	***
Bonds	LKFIX	Bonds	$247 million	1997	**
Small Cap	LKSCX	Stocks	$239 million	1994	**
Small-Mid Cap	LKSMX	Stocks	$17 million	2011	*

The Timothy Plan offers ten different funds, with total assets of approximately $1 billion. These different front-load funds are seen in table 30.4. Rear-load funds that charge sales fees over time are also available, as can be seen on the fund's website.

Table 30.4
Timothy Plan

Name	Symbol	Holdings	Assets	Begun	Ranking
Aggressive Growth	TAAGX	Stocks	$32 million	2000	*
Conservative Growth	TCGAX	Stocks	$48 million	2000	**
Defensive Strategies	TPDAX	Stocks	$47 million	2009	n/a
International	TPIAX	Stocks	$43 million	2007	*
Large/Mid Growth	TLGAX	Stocks	$107 million	2000	**
Large/Mid Value	TLVAX	Stocks	$229 million	1999	***
Small Cap	TPLNX	Stocks	$160 million	1994	**
Strategic Growth	TSGAX	Stocks	$39 million	2000	**
Fixed Income	TFIAX	Bonds	$79 million	1999	**
High Yield Bond	TPHAX	Bonds	$55 million	2007	*
Growth/Income	TGCIX	Stocks, bonds	$34 million	2013	*
Emerging Markets	TPECX	Stocks	$20 million	2012	*
Israel Common Values	TPCIX	Stocks	$104 million	2007	*

As you can see, there exists a wide variety of Catholic-oriented funds to consider. With some effort, an investor can find those that have appropriate objectives for any situation.

Monitoring Investments

Monitoring your investments is an important task.

Now that we have visited the various avenues available for investing, we turn to the monitoring of your portfolio. First, let us consider some general guidelines for individual securities management and then those for investing in mutual funds.

With a portfolio of individual stocks and bonds, it is prudent to review the holdings once or twice yearly. It has been the author's observation that investors tend to worry and oftentimes trade securities unnecessarily if they focus too much on a portfolio.

Nonetheless, if, upon review, a particular investment in a portfolio fails to meet the criteria for holding it, then a replacement must be selected. Also, if a particular investment appreciates substantially relative to the other holdings, then a portion of the position might be sold and the proceeds invested elsewhere. In another vein, should one experience a financial windfall such as a gift or inheritance, the proceeds must be allocated in a way that is consistent with one's objectives.

It should be noted that over the years, much research has shown that on balance neither individual investors nor professionals accurately time getting into or out of the market.[1] In fact, frequent trading usually results in unnecessary expenses and lost opportunity for most investors. Contrary to what is often espoused

---

[1] Seth C. Anderson, *Investment Management and Mismanagement: History, Findings, and Analysis* (New York: Springer, 2006), 57, 86.

in the popular media, a long-term "buy and hold" strategy tends to serve most investors best. Thus, we must not forget that one's investment objective usually changes only gradually as we grow older or as our situation changes. Obviously, monitoring requires time and effort; hence many investors turn to mutual funds to simplify matters.

Mutual funds require less monitoring than portfolios of individual securities because each fund has its own stated objective to which it must adhere under Securities Exchange Commission rules. Still, over a period of years, one needs to reallocate the proportion of individual funds within a portfolio. For example, a 35-year-old investor might hold a portfolio with 80 percent in two or more stock funds and 20 percent in a bond fund. When the investor turns 50, the individual will need to rebalance the portfolio to perhaps a 50 percent stock and 50 percent bond/safety blend.[2]

---

[2] This ratio assumes that you are married with children but may not take into account other factors. Please consult a financial professional for advice about your specific situation.

If You Become Unable to
Manage Your Investments

Who will manage your investments if you become unable to do so?

My father managed his own assets until his death at age 81. However, many people become incapable of handling this important task prior to their death. Thus, an important question is "*Who* will perform this function if this situation arises?"

Perhaps you have a spouse, relative, friend, or financial professional who could assume this responsibility. If so, you are fortunate to have someone on whom to rely. Nonetheless, you need to provide guidance for this individual by having in place documents containing general instructions and stated objectives for managing your portfolio.

There are two primary benefits of having written instructions. The first is to make the responsible party's tasks more manageable. The second is that of having the portfolio invested in a manner consistent with your objectives.

In my work as an expert witness, I have often seen incapacitated investors' funds mismanaged by financial professionals, friends, and family members. Sometimes the mismanagement resulted from dishonesty. At other times, it resulted from a lack of investment acumen. Regardless of the reason, the outcome was financial distress.

The upside of using a financial professional or someone close to you can be the individual attention provided. The downside is that individuals may become unable to continue in their fiduciary capacity for a variety of reasons. Thus, an alternative to individual management is that of a bank trust department.

The upside of using a trust department is its continuity: even if the bank goes out of business, the trust assets will be managed by a surviving entity. Also, the bank is obligated to operate within any reasonable guidelines established by the trust document that you sign. The downside perceived by some people is that your assets will be in the hands of an impersonal entity. Another downside is that the bank will often charge an annual fee, around 3 percent of total assets for more modest accounts. Yes, a trust department is an impersonal entity with a price tag attached, but the people working there are professionals who can be helpful. Based on my observations, a bank trust department is usually a better choice than an individual. You will need to shop around to find a department you can work with.

The Fruits of Your Investments
After Your Death

A person's life passes suddenly like a shadow.
—Thomas à Kempis, *The Imitation of Christ*

What will become of your assets after your death? This has been a question for many since antiquity. Some people simply ignore the question and let their survivors deal with the issue.[1] This is one solution, but it is not the best one. Sirach 33:23–24 directs us to tend to our affairs and to distribute what we have when we die:

> 23 Keep control over all your affairs; let no one tarnish your glory.
>
> 24 When your few days reach their limit, at the time of death distribute your inheritance.

As discussed in the prior chapter, perhaps you have a spouse, relative, friend, or financial professional who can assist in the distribution of your estate. If so, you are fortunate. Nonetheless, you need to provide directives to this individual by having guidelines (such as your will) containing clear instructions. Such direction is seen in Tobit 4:1–3,20:

---

[1] For a more general discussion of how to relieve your heirs of the details of your personal matters and funeral arrangements, see the appendix of *Remember to Live* by Thomas Ryan (New York: Paulist Press, 2012).

1 That same day Tobit remembered the money he had deposited with Gabael at Rages in Media, and he thought,

2 "Now that I have asked for death, why should I not call my son Tobiah and let him know about this money before I die?"

3 So he called his son Tobiah; and when he came, he said to him: "My son, when I die, give me a decent burial. Honor your mother, and do not abandon her as long as she lives. Do whatever pleases her, and do not grieve her spirit in any way."

20 "And now, son, I wish to inform you that I have deposited a great sum of money with Gabri's son Gavael at Rages in Media ..."

As discussed in the prior chapter, the upside of getting help from a financial professional or someone close to you can be the individual attention they give. However, this individual may become unable to continue in this capacity for a variety of reasons. Thus, as seen previously, an alternative to an individual manager is a bank trust department.

A trust department is obligated to operate within any reasonable guidelines established by your will and by any other documents you sign. The employment of a trust department can be extremely beneficial. For example, if there is a young beneficiary involved, a trust can be established and managed for the welfare of this individual. Additionally, a trust can be useful when a beneficiary is incapacitated in any way, or simply cannot responsibly manage assets.

There are various trust structures for different purposes, and trust departments can help in selecting the appropriate one. Once the needs of all beneficiaries have been met, the trust can be liquidated and distributed according to your wishes. We are blessed to have legal and institutional structures to help us with the final disposition and good use of our God-given assets.

34

Closing

*"Since we know the way we have to take to please God—
namely, that of keeping His commandments and counsels—
let us be very diligent in doing this, and in meditating
upon His life and death, and upon all that we owe Him ..."*
—Teresa of Ávila, *Interior Castle*

I hope this book proves to be as beneficial to you, dear reader, as writing it has been for me. It has helped me appreciate how I, as a Catholic, am to be disposed toward my investing responsibilities.

As discussed in part I, each of us should give thanks to God for our assets and be good stewards of them. In doing so, we are to avoid greed, and we are to be prudent and temperate in our investment endeavors. As well, we must follow Saint Pio's prescription for eternal health to pray, hope, and not worry. After all, Matthew 6:25–27 tells us:

> 25 "Therefore I tell you, do not worry about your life, what you will eat (or drink), or about your body, what you will wear. Is not life more than food and the body more than clothing?

> 26 Look at the birds in the sky; they do not sow or reap, they gather nothing into barns, yet your heavenly Father feeds them. Are not you more important than they?

27 Can any of you by worrying add a single moment
to your life-span?

In managing our financial resources, we must simply use good judgment while adhering to the Church's two principles of stewardship, which are: (1) obtaining a reasonable market-based rate of return, and (2) implementing investment strategies based on Catholic moral teachings. By doing so, we can attain success with our investment endeavors and be in a better position to touch human life, both now and over the long term in serving our Lord. "For from him and through him and for him are all things. To him be glory forever. Amen" (Romans 11:36).

References

The American Heritage Dictionary of the English Language. New York: American Heritage Publishing Co., Inc. 1969.

Anderson, Seth C. *Investment Management and Mismanagement: History, Findings, and Analysis.* New York: Springer, 2006.

Catholic Church. *Catechism of the Catholic Church.* 2nd ed. Washington, DC: United States Catholic Conference, 1997.

CatholicReference.net. "Prudence." This site contains the *Modern Catholic Dictionary* by Fr. John Hardon. Accessed November 14, 2009. http://www.catholicreference.net/index.cfm.

de Sales, St. Francis. *Introduction to the Devout Life.* Rockford, IL: Tan Books and Publishers, 1990.

ewtn.com. "Padre Pio: The Man—Biography." Accessed September 28, 2009. http://www.ewtn.com/padrepio/man/biography2.htm.

Grisez, Germain. *The Way of the Lord: Difficult Moral Questions.* Vol. 3. New York: St. Paul's/Alba House, 1997.

Ibbotson Associates. *Stocks, Bonds, Bills, and Inflation: 2016 Yearbook.* Chicago: Ibbotson Associates, 2016.

Kempis, Thomas à. *The Imitation of Christ.* New York: Catholic Book Publishing Co., 1985.

Krooss, Herman E., and Martin R. Blyn. *History of Financial Intermediaries.* New York: Random House, 1971.

Kuebler, Daniel. "The Mess Money Made." *National Catholic Register,* May 10–16, 2009.

Murphy, Charles. "The Good Life from a Catholic Perspective: The Problem of Consumption." Accessed December 23, 2009.

http://www.squidinkbooks.com/omosclc/ppt/Creation/ Good.Life.pdf.

New Advent. "Prudence." Father Rickaby was a British Jesuit of the pre–World War I era. This site contains the *Catholic Encyclopedia*. Accessed June 14, 2012. http://www. newadvent.org/cathen/12517b.htm.

New American Bible. New York: Catholic Book Publishing Co., 1992.

Office for Social Justice. "Economic Justice for All." Accessed August 16, 2018. http://www.osjspm.org/economic_justice_for_all. aspx.

Pronechen, Joseph. "Pray, Hope and Don't Worry." *National Catholic Register*, September 20–26, 2009.

Ryan, Thomas. *Remember to Live*. New York: Paulist Press, 2012.

Teresa of Ávila. *The Interior Castle*. New York: Doubleday, 2004.

United States Conference of Catholic Bishops. "Socially Responsible Investment Guidelines." Accessed August 15, 2010. http:// www.usccb.org/finance/srig.shtml.

Williamson, Gordon. *Getting Started in Annuities*. Hoboken, NJ: John Wiley and Sons, 1998.

Printed in the United States
by Baker & Taylor Publisher Services